Celebrating Black History

Errol Lloyd

OXFORD
UNIVERSITY PRESS

OXFORD
UNIVERSITY PRESS

is a department of the University of Oxford.
It furthers the University's objective of excellence in research, scholarship,
and education by publishing worldwide in

Oxford   New York
Auckland   Cape Town   Dar es Salaam   Hong Kong   Karachi
Kuala Lumpur   Madrid   Melbourne   Mexico City   Nairobi
New Delhi   Shanghai   Taipei   Toronto

With offices in

Argentina   Austria   Brazil   Chile   Czech Republic   France   Greece
Guatemala   Hungary   Italy   Japan   Poland   Portugal   Singapore
South Korea   Switzerland   Thailand   Turkey   Ukraine   Vietnam

Oxford is a registered trade mark of Oxford University Press
in the UK and in certain other countries

Text © Errol Lloyd 2007

The moral rights of the author have been asserted

Database right Oxford University Press (maker)

First published 2007

All rights reserved. No part of this publication may be reproduced,
stored in a retrieval system, or transmitted, in any form or by any means,
without the prior permission in writing of Oxford University Press,
or as expressly permitted by law, or under terms agreed with the appropriate
reprographics rights organization. Enquiries concerning reproduction
outside the scope of the above should be sent to the Rights Department,
Oxford University Press, at the address above

You must not circulate this book in any other binding or cover
and you must impose this same condition on any acquirer

British Library Cataloguing in Publication Data

Data available

ISBN: 978-0-19-846125-8

1 3 5 7 9 10 8 6 4 2

Printed in China

Paper used in the production of this book is a natural,
recyclable product made from wood grown in sustainable forests.
The manufacturing process conforms to the environmental
regulations of the country of origin

Acknowledgements

The publisher would like to thank the following for permission to reproduce photographs: **p5&6** British Library/akg-images; **p7** National Maritime Museum, London; **p8** National Portrait Gallery/Getty Images; **p9**t Mary Evans Picture Library/Alamy, **p9**b Christie's Images; **p10**t Corbis UK Ltd., **p10**b David J. & Janice L. Frent Collection/Corbis UK Ltd.; **p11** Jacques M. Chenet/Corbis UK Ltd.; **p12**t Print Collection, Miriam and Ira D. Wallach Division of Art, Prints and Photographs/The New York Public Library, Astor, Lenox and Tillden Foundations, **p12**b The Gleaner Company Limited, 1976./Jamaica Gleaner; **p13** Allsport Hulton/Getty Images; **p14**t Fred Ramage/Keystone/Hulton Archive/Getty Images, **p14**b Hulton Archive/Getty Images; **p15** BBC Photograph Library; **p16** Bettmann/Corbis UK Ltd.; **p17**t Burt Shavitz/Pix Inc./Time Life Pictures/Getty Images, **p17**b TopFoto; **p18**t Rebecca Cook/Reuters/Corbis UK Ltd., **p18**b Gene Herrick/Associated Press/PA Photos; **p19**t Bettmann/Corbis UK Ltd., **p19**b Brendan Smialowski/EPA/Corbis UK Ltd.; **p20**t Donald Uhrbrock/Time Life Pictures/Getty Images, **p20**b TopFoto; **p21**t&b Bettmann/Corbis UK Ltd.; **p22** UWC – Robben Island Mayibuye Archives; **p23**t David Turnley/Corbis UK Ltd., **p23**b Louise Gubb/The Image Works/TopFoto

Cover photograph: Corbis/Hulton-Deutsch collection

Illustrations by Martin Sanders/Beehive Illustrations: **p5**, **p8**

Contents

Introduction **4**

Olaudah Equiano **6**

Mary Seacole **8**

Marcus Garvey **10**

C.L.R. James **12**

Una Marson **14**

Malcolm X **16**

Rosa Parks **18**

Martin Luther King, Jr **20**

Nelson Mandela **22**

Glossary and Index **24**

Introduction

In the 16th century, many people set sail from Europe for the newly discovered lands of America and the Caribbean. Some went in search of riches and adventure, and others went to escape from religious **persecution**.

They set up plantations and grew crops like coffee, cotton, sugar cane and tobacco. There was a shortage of workers, so the Europeans forced the local people to work on their plantations. But the local people soon died out from the harsh treatment they received.

The European settlers then brought servants over from Europe. This didn't solve the problem either, because the servants only came for a short time.

Eventually, the Europeans turned to Africa, and over the next four hundred years, millions of Africans were transported across the Atlantic in chains and sold as slaves. Slaves were thought of as property and were usually treated harshly. Many rebelled or ran away.

This book is about some of the many outstanding black leaders of the past three hundred years.

> Although slavery was **abolished** over a hundred and fifty years ago, much of modern black history has continued to be a struggle for freedom and equality.

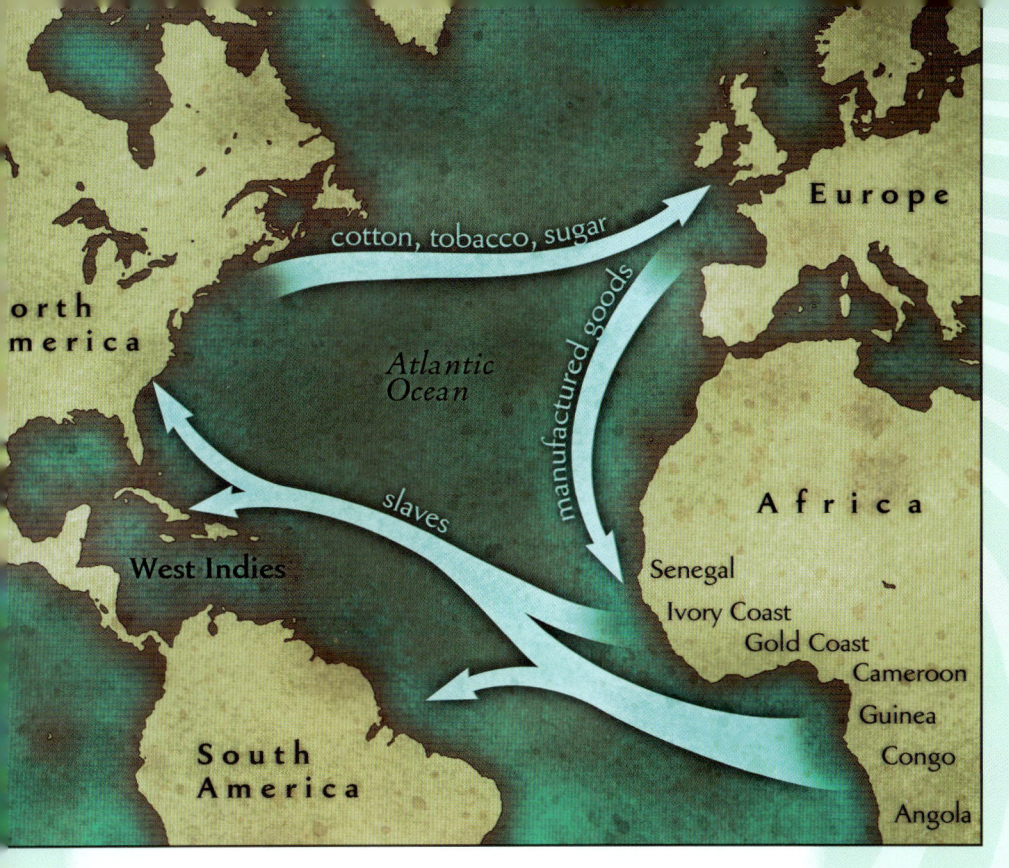

Triangular Trade: Ships left Europe with goods to be sold in Africa. The ships took Africans to be sold as slaves in the Caribbean and the Americas. Then they returned to Europe with goods like sugar, tobacco and cotton.

In the Caribbean island of Haiti, Toussaint L'Ouverture led the slaves in a revolt. They defeated the armies of Napoleon, the British and the Spanish, and set up a free **republic** in 1802.

Olaudah Equiano
(1745–1797)

Equiano was born in Guinea, Africa. He was kidnapped as a child and transported to America on a slave ship. He was sold to an officer of the Royal Navy while Britain was at war with France, and Olaudah's job was to carry gunpowder up to the guns on deck during battles. Between sea voyages, he learnt to read and write.

At the end of the war he thought he would be rewarded by money and his freedom. Instead, his master sold him to another sea captain who took him to the Caribbean island of Montserrat. He was then sold to a kind Quaker who gave him a responsible job because he could read and write.

Olaudah became rich and famous as a result of his book.

He managed to earn enough money over the next four years to buy his own freedom. He returned to England and worked as a seaman, travelling the world.

Olaudah took part in an expedition to find a sea route to India via the North Pole. He had many adventures and was saved from drowning.

Olaudah married an Englishwoman, Susanna Cullen, in 1792 and they had two daughters.

He was horrified by the cruelties of slavery in the Caribbean and wrote a powerful anti-slavery book which became an international best seller. Although he died ten years before the British slave trade was abolished, his book played a very important part in bringing this about.

Mary Seacole
(1805–1881)

Mary Seacole was a Jamaican nurse who had great success in treating cholera, yellow fever and other diseases in Jamaica, Panama and Cuba.

When the **Crimean War** broke out in Europe in 1853, she travelled to England because she wanted to go to Turkey to help Florence Nightingale.

The Crimea is in the south of Russia near Turkey.

Mary Seacole was often compared to Florence Nightingale and was sometimes called 'The Black Florence Nightingale'.

The War Office refused her an interview because she was black and they did not believe she was a skilled nurse. She travelled to the Crimea anyway and set up her own headquarters near the battlefields.

She would often go out on to the battlefield to nurse sick and wounded soldiers during the danger of battle.

Mary Seacole called the soldiers she cared for her 'sons', and they called her 'Mother Seacole'. She was given many awards for her services.

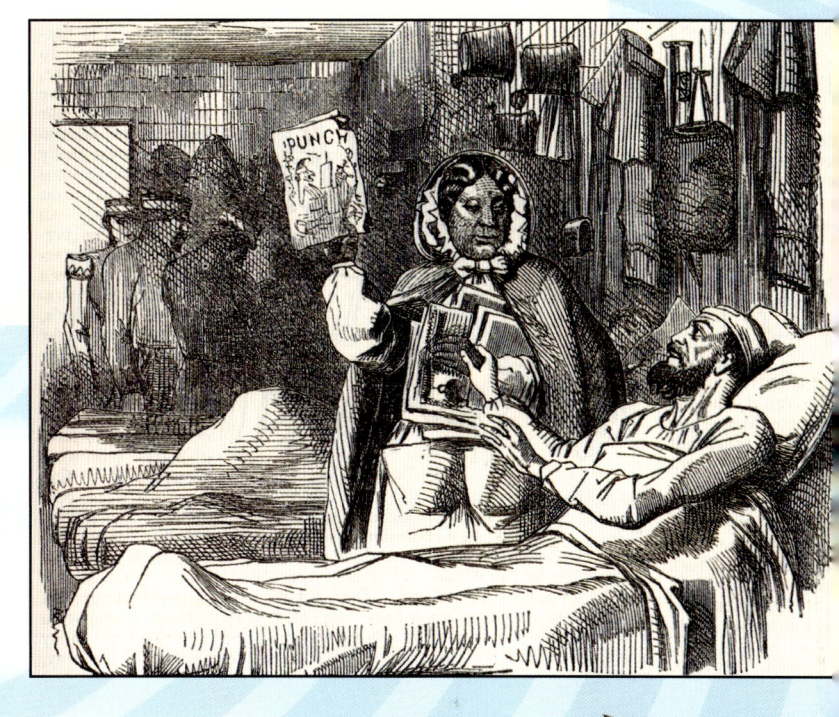

When the war ended, she returned to England with no money and in poor health. But many people came to her aid, including military commanders, members of the royal family and ordinary people. They staged a grand military festival at the Royal Surrey Gardens over four nights to raise money for her.

Mary Seacole died in 1881 and is buried at St Mary's Catholic Cemetery, in North West London.

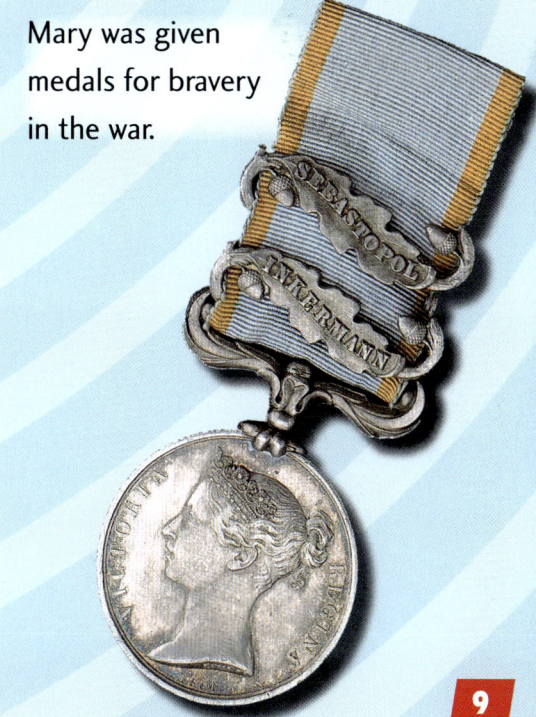

Mary was given medals for bravery in the war.

Marcus Garvey
(1887–1940)

Marcus Garvey was born in Jamaica, which was a British **colony** at the time.

As a young man, he travelled throughout the Caribbean and Central America. He saw that black people, everywhere, were living in poverty. This was shocking because slavery had been abolished for over fifty years.

Marcus Garvey worked as a journalist in London from 1912–1914.

He thought that the only way to improve their condition was to unite all black people into one strong group. He formed an organisation called the United Negro Improvement Association (UNIA) which stood for black self-respect and unity.

In a short time UNIA became the largest black organisation in history, with over a thousand branches in Africa, the Caribbean, Central America and the United States.

Garvey died in England in 1940. He is still regarded as a great champion of black freedom, even though his 'Back to Africa' movement did not win great support.

Marcus Garvey's portrait is honoured by African-Americans at the Million Man March in 1995.

When Jamaica became independent in 1962, he was named the first National Hero of Jamaica. Today he is honoured in many other countries as well.

Garvey Quotes:

"A people without the knowledge of their past history, origin and culture is like a tree without roots."

"If you have no confidence in self, you are twice defeated in the race of life. But with confidence you have won before you have started."

C.L.R. James
(1901–1989)

Cyril Lionel Robert James was born in Trinidad in 1901 and left for England in 1932.

He did not agree with Marcus Garvey that black people could solve their problems by going back to Africa. He believed that black and white workers should act together to bring about change, but he also thought that black people could have their own independent organisations.

C.L.R. James **campaigned** with his boyhood friend, George Padmore, to free African and Caribbean colonies from British rule.

His lectures and articles about art, sport, politics, popular culture and world problems made him internationally famous.

C.L.R. James as a young man.

C.L.R. James addressing a mass rally in Kingston, Jamaica. The Jamaican Prime Minister, Michael Manley, is seated on his left.

He wrote many important books on politics, literature and sport. He believed that cricket had a lot to teach about life, such as discipline, sportsmanship and honesty, and his most famous book was about cricket, called *Beyond a Boundary*. Many people thought it was the finest book ever written about sport.

C.L.R. James died in London in 1989.

Sir Frank Worrell was already a great batsman when he was appointed captain of the West Indies team.

Between 1958 and 1962, C.L.R. James returned to Trinidad to edit a national newspaper. The newspaper campaigned for Frank Worrell, a black man, to be made captain of the West Indies cricket team. Up until then the team was always led by white captains, even if they were not the best qualified. Worrell was appointed, and went on to become a great captain. He was knighted by the Queen and became Sir Frank Worrell.

Una Marson
(1905–1965)

Una Marson was born in Jamaica in 1905. She lived a varied and interesting life.

She arrived in England in 1932 and worked for an organisation to help black people who were newly settled in Britain. She became a well known **feminist**, fighting discrimination against black women, especially in the nursing profession.

Una Marson is the author of four books of poetry and three plays.

Later she became secretary to Haile Selassie, the emperor of Ethiopia. In 1936 she accompanied him to the League of Nations to protest against the invasion of his country by Italy.

Haile Selassie was claimed to be a descendant of King Solomon and the Queen of Sheba (Ethiopia), mentioned in the Bible.

She was the first black woman programme maker for the BBC from 1939–1946. Her wartime broadcasts to the Caribbean kept West Indians in England in touch with their families back home. They also helped to promote West Indian literature.

Una Marson was one of the first women poets of the Caribbean. Her colleagues at the BBC included famous writers such as George Orwell and T.S. Eliot.

She worked in Israel in the 1960s after the Israeli Prime Minister, Golda Meir, invited her to work there.

She set up the Jamaican *Save the Children Fund* to help lift deprived children out of poverty.

Malcolm X
(1925–1965)

Malcolm Little, later to be known as Malcolm X, was born in 1925 in the south of America.

He had a tough childhood. White racists burnt down his family house and later murdered his father. His mother was driven insane and Malcolm, without parents to guide him, ended up in prison.

While he was in prison, Malcolm copied one page from the dictionary each day to learn new words. He also read encyclopaedias and many other books.

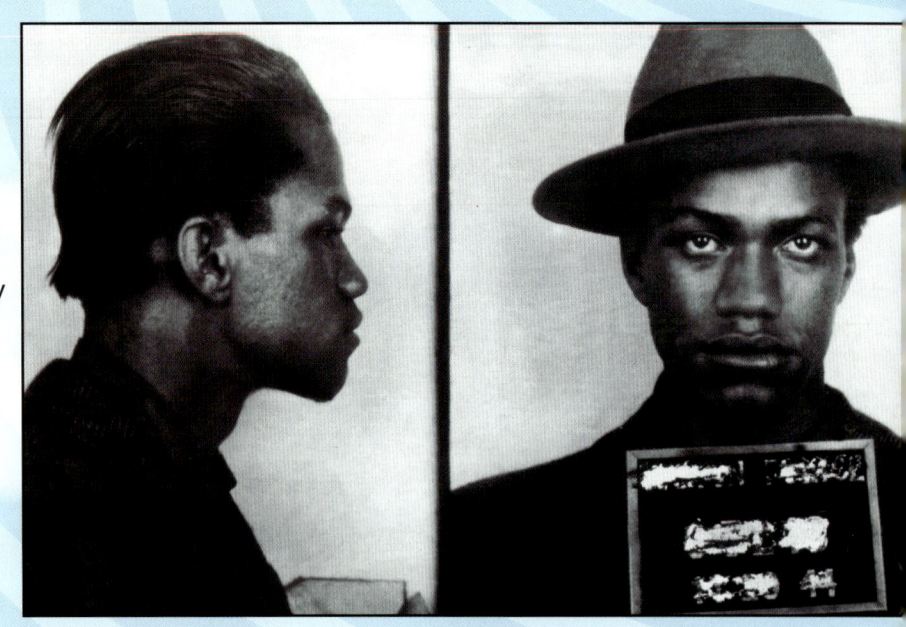

In prison, he joined a group called the Nation of Islam. They believed that white people were devils and black people were **Allah's** chosen people. Members were not allowed to drink or smoke.

Malcolm started to live a disciplined life. He read widely and educated himself.

When he was released from prison, he became a minister of the Nation of Islam. He attracted many new members by his personal **charisma**, his gift for public speaking and his **militancy**.

Although he did not preach violence, Malcolm believed that black people had the right to defend themselves if they were attacked by white people.

A turning point in Malcolm X's life came when he made a pilgrimage to **Mecca** in Saudi Arabia – the religious capital of Islam. There he saw black and white people mingling together in harmony. He changed many of his earlier beliefs about race and left the Nation of Islam to set up his own **mosque**.

He was **assassinated** in 1965 by gunmen who accused him of betraying the Nation of Islam.

After his trip to Mecca and the Middle East and Africa, Malcolm said: 'My friends today are black, brown, red, yellow and *white*!'

Rosa Parks
(1913–2005)

Montgomery is a city in the southern state of Alabama, United States of America. Alabama's strict **segregation** laws did not allow black and white people to marry one another, go to the same schools, use the same restaurants or even play games, like cards or football, together.

One law said that black people had to sit at the back of city buses. What's more, they had to give up their seat to a white person if the seats at the front were full.

One day in December 1955, Rosa Parks refused to give up her seat to a white man. She was arrested and fined in court.

Rosa Parks having her fingerprints taken after her arrest.

Rosa was a member of the National Association for the Advancement of Coloured People (NAACP). They took her case to the Supreme Court. In the meantime, black people refused to use the city buses at all.

In 1956, the Supreme Court ruled that the decision of the Montgomery court was unfair and against the United States constitution (the laws which state how the USA is to be governed).

After the Supreme Court decision, black people were able to sit anywhere they liked on buses anywhere in the United States.

It was a great triumph, and Rosa Parks has often been called the Mother of the Civil Rights Movement for the example she set.

The President of the USA at the funeral of Rosa Parks in 2005.

Bibliography

Rosa Parks: My Story
An autobiography aimed at younger readers

19

Martin Luther King, Jr.
(1929–1968)

Martin Luther King Junior was a Baptist minister, born in Atlanta, Georgia, in 1929.

In 1954 Martin moved to Montgomery, Alabama. A year later, Rosa Parks was arrested for refusing to give up her bus seat to a white man.

Martin Luther King with his wife Coretta, and two of their four children.

In 1964, Martin Luther King was awarded the **Nobel Peace Prize** for his non-violent campaign for civil rights in America. Aged 35, he was the youngest person ever to receive the prize.

Martin organised Rosa Parks' appeal to the US Supreme Court, as well as the **boycott** of the Montgomery city buses. For almost a year, black people walked everywhere or shared cars. Eventually the bus company was forced to allow people to sit wherever they liked.

Martin, a **devout** Christian, believed that only non-violent means should be used to challenge unjust laws. As part of a **civil disobedience** campaign, he led marches for civil and voting rights in spite of assaults and death threats. He was assassinated on 4 April, 1968.

Martin Luther King became leader of the Civil Rights Movement. In 1963 he led the great 'March on Washington for Jobs and Freedom.' He delivered his famous 'I have a dream' speech, to a crowd of over 250,000 black and white people, and millions watching on television. The speech set out his vision of an America free from racial injustice. The following year President Johnson signed the Civil Rights Act, which guaranteed black people equal rights.

President Lyndon Johnson shakes hands with Martin Luther King after signing the Civil Rights Act. He gave Martin his pen and Martin called it "my most precious possession".

Nelson Mandela

Born 1918

In 1948, the white government of South Africa passed the **apartheid** laws to separate the races living there. Whites were not allowed to marry black or non-white people, live in the same areas, go to the same schools or use the same buses. Only white people could vote.

Nelson Mandela was born in 1918 in a village. He spent a peaceful childhood looking after cattle. His father was a counsellor to the Thembu royal family, and when he died, Nelson was 'adopted' by the royal family. But, to escape an arranged marriage, he ran away to Johannesburg and became a lawyer.

He later became one of the main leaders of the African National Congress (ANC). He organised demonstrations and fought so strongly against the Apartheid laws that the white government arrested and sentenced him to life imprisonment.

This photograph of Nelson Mandela was taken while he was a prisoner on Robben Island, near Cape Town.

In 1990, after twenty-seven years in prison, Nelson Mandela was released. In 1994 he was elected President of South Africa in free elections in which black people could vote for the first time. He stepped down in 1997.

Nelson Mandela later returned to visit his cell on Robben Island.

After his release from prison, Nelson Mandela helped to bring black and white South Africans together in a spirit of forgiveness. He was awarded the Nobel Peace prize in 1993 and is admired and respected throughout the world.

What Nelson Mandela said at his trial made him the symbol of the dream of a free, democratic South Africa:

"I have fought against white domination, and I have fought against black domination. I have cherished the ideal of a democratic and free society in which all persons live together in harmony and with equal opportunities. It is an ideal I hope to live for and to achieve. But if needs be, it is an ideal for which I am prepared to die."

Glossary

abolish – to end by law
Allah – the Muslim term for God
apartheid – a policy enforced to separate white and black people
assassination – to murder a political or public figure
boycott – a complete ban on doing something
campaign – a planned series of actions
charisma – the special quality that makes a person popular
civil disobedience – refusing to obey a law without using violence
colony – an area of land that people of another country settle in and control
Crimean War – the 1854–1856 war between Russia and other countries in the Balkans

devout – sincere, deeply religious
feminist – a person who strongly supports equal rights for women
Mecca – Islam's holiest place
militancy – being prepared to fight
mosque – a place where Muslims worship
Nobel Peace Prize – a prize awarded to a person for promoting peace between peoples
persecution – ill treatment
proclaim – to announce publicly
republic – a country which is ruled by the people rather than by royalty
segregation – the separation of different racial groups

Index

apartheid   22
Crimean War   8, 9
Haiti   5
Jamaica   8, 10, 11, 14, 15
Montgomery   18, 19, 20
Montserrat   6
plantations   4
servants   4
slavery   5, 6, 7
South Africa   22, 23
triangular trade   5
Trinidad   12